Be You!
COOKBOOK

To: Momma B

For always teaching, inspiring and

encouraging me to chase my wildest dreams

to the moon and back.

What's the Buzz?

My obsession with cooking sparked as a kid with a curious mind. I wouldn't just eat my food; I would examine it. I wondered how in the world yogurt came from milk or why my Goldfish crackers we're always perfectly smiling at me. I remember taking anything from the pantry and mixing it together to see what it would taste like. Transforming to a mad scientist after school, I would pride myself in what I called "my concoctions." The chemistry of Gushers melting in the microwave and dipping salty-sweet goldfish and yogurt combinations were just the beginning. Over the next 20 years, I sophisticated my culinary works but never lost the love for using my imagination with food.

I studied food, worked with food, even made art from food, until I was head-over-heels in love with this very simple yet complex idea of food. Discovering the culture, art, and emotion that goes into cooking is my favorite game. An important ground rule to this game includes devotedly caring for your ingredients to give your recipes a unique connection. It provides flavor so particular that when you taste it, it makes you think, "ahh… It tastes like home." Once your foundation is pure and stable, let your freedom of flavor shine.

Introspectively, cooking is a beautiful way to learn about one's self. In this book, each recipe reflects a story, an important part of my memoir. I developed the recipes from special journeys around the Midwest, West Coast, and sporadic travel. I am constantly chasing flavors to create my culinary diary.

My journey helped create a stunning menu for my first restaurant, *The Honey B.* A honey bee is much like a chef in the back of a kitchen, often unnoticed but extremely vital to the food we eat. Bees come together to pollinate our food. Similarly, it's a chef's duty to spread the importance of sustainable cooking. My tiny, rapidly evolving café is inspired by my love for our hard working bees. It also happens to be my favorite outlet to my culinary manifestation.

The *Be You Cookbook* is a collection of my recipes harmonizing with my imagination in hopes to inspire mindful creativity with food. To me, a chef sharing their recipes is an artist showing off their art gallery. Aside from the medium used, I think of cooking similar to my paintings. Each recipe has a little animal I painted specifically for that page as a reminder to provoke your creativity while cooking.

My recipes are not intended to meticulously follow, but rather to have fun with. Don't be afraid to explore flavors that fascinate you personally. Replace a fruit or a spice for one that you like. Get lost on a wild adventure with flavors healthy and local to your community. And most importantly, *be you!*

CONTENTS

Good Morning Bee-utiful!

CARROT CAKE PARFAIT

Cake for breakfast? Yes, please! Carrot cake is the new granola for this decadent parfait. Initially invented to recycle a batch of lopsided muffins, it's now my all-time favorite way to pair yogurt. Never be afraid to recycle your old recipes, you may just discover a new one.

For this recipe, I reshaped my favorite carrot cake recipe into muffins, and then into this parfait. The cold, creamy yogurt paired with warm, fluffy cake, and added pistachios for a little crunch creates something fun to wake up on the right side of the bed with.

Directions:

1. Preheat the oven to 350 degrees.

2. In a stand mixer, cream together the butter and sugar. Add one egg at a time.

3. In a separate bowl, mix the flour, baking powder, cinnamon, and salt.

4. Slowly add the flour mixture to the other ingredients.

5. Fold in grated carrots and pistachios.

6. Pour batter into lined muffin tins and bake for approximately 15 minutes.

7. Gently crumble the warm muffins and layer with your favorite Greek yogurt and a few chopped pistachios.

Ingredients:

1 cup vegetable oil

2 cups granulated sugar

3 eggs

4 cups carrots, grated

2 cups all-purpose flour

2 tsp baking powder

2 tsp cinnamon

1 tsp salt

1 cup pistachios, + garnish

2 cups your favorite yogurt

Be Different

Bee Tip: For even more carrot cake flare, whip a few tablespoons of cream cheese into the yogurt.

MATCHA SMOOTHIE BOWL

My days often qualify for a healthy dose of caffeine. An antioxidant-packed Matcha bowl paired with a cup of joe is one of my top 'breakfast of champions' meals. I flow with positive energy after a well-rounded breakfast like this one. It's important to note, when working around people all day, good energy can reflect off your co-workers too. So, think about eating a solid breakfast for yourself and for your neighbor too! Matcha in particular, is an interesting super food. This ancient ingredient praised upon by Zen masters brings a grounded alertness and clarity to your mind. Dense in antioxidants, metabolism boosting, calming, detoxifying, rich in vitamins, reduces cholesterol, and tastes great. Woah! Yes, please!

Directions:

1. Mix everything in a blender on high speed until smooth and creamy.
2. Garnish with your favorite fruits, nuts, and seeds.

Bee Tip: Chia seeds act as a wonderful natural roux, making for a perfect (healthy) thickening agent in many types of sauces. If you don't have frozen fruit, it can help make your smoothies nice and thick too!

Ingredients:

1 cup coconut milk or
coconut water

1/4 cup frozen spinach

2 tsp matcha green tea
powder

1 frozen banana

1/2 cup frozen mango

1 lemon, juice and zest

Toppings

favorite fruit, nuts,
and seeds

Be
Energetic

HONEY B TOAST

Even if you think you could never find time or talent to make the same quality bread you buy, I encourage you to just try this bread recipe once. Important notes to making crave worthy bread are having fresh ingredients and the right ratios. There's actually even a term called baker's math.

To not complicate things, simply feel by working with your hands. Physically touching dough is a great way to determine the next step. Every dough is completely different. For this dough, focus on slowly incorporating the last few cups of flour until the dough starts to pull together but is still slightly sticky to the touch. Creating a special bread is as easy as tuning in and getting intimate with what baking feels like.

Directions:

1. In a stand mixer, add the water, yeast, and honey. Let rest for a few minutes.
2. Add the salt and slow incorporate the flour. Use just enough until the dough starts to pull away from the bowl.
3. Transfer the dough to an oiled bowl and cover with plastic wrap or a towel. Let rise for 1-2 hours, or until doubled in size.
4. Preheat your oven to 150 degrees.
5. Oil your hands and punch down the dough. Shape the dough into a loaf pan and place it in the oven until it doubles in size, about 20 minutes.
6. Remove the bread from the oven and preheat the oven to 350 degrees.
7. Bake the bread at 350 for about 30 minutes, until golden brown.

Bee Tip: Try playing with the texture and flavor by adding different nuts, seeds, or dried fruits to your bread. Perhaps coconut flakes and dried mango, or pine nuts and sundried tomato

Ingredients:

2 cups warm water
(110 degrees)

1 ½ Tbsp active dry yeast

1/2 cup honey

2 tsp salt

8+/- cups whole wheat flour
(freshly ground is best!)

1 cup sunflower seeds

¼ cup black sesame seeds

CHEDDAR n' CHIVE
savory waffle sandwiches

Every weekend when I was a kid, my mom would let us choose either pancakes, waffles, or French toast for breakfast. I would naturally dive in to help out. Perhaps the beginning of my breakfast love affair. Second to my obsession for breakfast is my love for big, bold flavors, especially in cheese. The marriage of sharp cheddar and fresh chives with a tried-and-true waffle recipe has turned into a favorite Honey B recipe. Every ingredient besides the butter is a 1:1 ratio, making this is a perfect recipe to double for a stellar waffle party, or just a fail-proof recipe for an impressive brunch.

Directions:

1. In a large mixing bowl, whisk together the milk and eggs. Slowly stir in the melted butter.
2. Stir in the grated cheese, flour, baking powder, salt, and chives.
3. Press batter on a greased waffle iron for 3-5 minutes. Enjoy while they're hot!

Bee Tip: Interchange cheeses and other savory flavors in the waffle for endless gourmet infused waffles. Perhaps blue cheese and caramelized onions folded into the batter. Yum!

Ingredients:

2 cups whole milk

2 eggs

1/2 cup butter, melted

2 cups grated sharp cheddar

2 cups flour

2 tsp baking powder

2 tsp salt

1/2 cup chopped chives

HEIRLOOM TOMATO TART

with lemon and ricotta

After being spoiled with local heirloom tomatoes, it's hard to enjoy any other type. Every Tuesday and Saturday, I religiously stock up on Belly Lik' farms juicy tomatoes for the café. Sometimes they're almost too pretty to eat. Vibrant, freshly picked tomatoes in a buttery pastry dough makes for a sexy, nearly effortless breakfast recipe.

A lesson I've learned and loved while playing with food is you don't have to make food look impressive, you can let the ingredients impress you. Tomatoes develop different flavor identities when grown in different types of soil. While in Italy, I discovered Naples grows first class tomatoes using volcanic-ash soil, but Santa Barbara's farmers do quite a fine job as well.

Bee Tip: Instead of shaping the tart in a pan, all the dough can be rolled out, stuffed with the filling, and folded up the sides to form a Galette, a free-form funky pie.

Ingredients:

<u>Pastry Dough</u>

2 cups all-purpose flour

½ tsp salt

2 tsp sugar

12 Tbsp butter, cubed

6-7 Tbsp ice water

<u>Filling</u>

4-5 heirloom tomatoes, thinly sliced

1 tsp salt

5 cloves garlic, minced

1 lemon, zest and juice

8 oz ricotta cheese

½ cup fresh basil

1 egg

salt and pepper, to taste

<u>Garnish</u>

fresh basil and

drizzled honey

Directions:

1. To make the pastry dough, pulse the flour, sugar, salt, and butter together in a food processor into pea-sized crumbs.

2. Slowly add ice water, until dough comes together but is not too sticky. Add more flour if needed.

3. Refrigerate at least 2 hours or overnight.

4. Meanwhile, slice the onions in half and then into 1/2 in strips. Cook on medium low heat with a few tbsp. of butter for about 30 minutes, until caramel in color.

5. Stir in the garlic, ricotta, fresh basil, salt, and pepper.

6. Preheat the oven to 350.

7. Roll out the refrigerated pastry dough into a 12 inch circle, 1/4 inch thick.

8. Press the rolled dough into a 10 inch springform pan.

9. Spread the ricotta mixture inside.

10. Neatly lay the sliced tomatoes in a spiral on top of the ricotta.

11. Trim any excess dough off the edges.

12. Bake for 25 min, until golden brown.

Photo Reference: page 97

Be local

EGG CASSEROLE

I have been making this breakfast dish each Christmas for my family for as long as I can remember. It started as a basic recipe I learned when I was younger. I scrambled together eggs and white bread and it slowly evolved with more love. In the Midwest, I grew up almost entirely off of casserole dishes. A pleasant, hodge-podge way to mix a bunch of yummy ingredients into one warm serving dish.

What makes this recipe so special is it opens my creativity. Each Christmas eve I specialize the recipe a little more, never making it exactly the same. I love how unique and versatile the properties of eggs are. You could continue to reinvent this recipe forever. Also a good explanation for the vague description of ingredients listed. I hope it opens your creativity too!

Directions:

1. Lightly butter a large casserole dish.
2. Beat the eggs and milk together. Fold in the remainder of the ingredients.
3. Pour into the casserole dish and refrigerate covered overnight.
4. In the morning, bake the casserole at 350 degrees for about 30-40 minutes.

Bee Tip: If you don't have a crowd to feed a dozen eggs, you can cut the recipe down or bake the mixture in muffin tins, freeze, reheat, and eat as little breakfast quiches.

Ingredients:

12 eggs

1 cup milk
(almond or whole)

1 cup your favorite
cheese
  -i.e. blue or feta

10 pieces your favorite bread
  -i.e. brioche or sourdough

2 cups mixed veggies
  -i.e. shiitakes and

spinach salt and

pepper, to taste

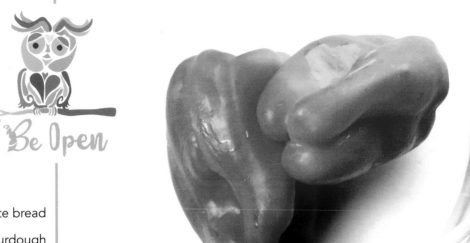

Be Open

LEMONADE BREAD

Growing up with blistering hot Chicago summers, I loved drinking my fair share of lemonade, and eating it too... This recipe was inspired while watching *Semi Homemade with Sandra Lee* after school as a kid. I loved how she would use random 'kid snack' foods in her recipes. I found myself using lemonade concentrate to bring out lemon in lots of recipes like this 'lazy' lemon bread. A sweet and tart recipe that sure hits the spot for a sugar tooth on a hot summer day.

Directions:

1. Preheat oven to 350 degrees.
2. Cream together the eggs, butter, and sugar. Add in 3 tbsp of concentrate and almond milk.
3. Stir in the flour, baking powder, and poppy seeds.
4. Pour batter into loaf pan and bake for about 20 min, until golden brown.
5. Remove from the oven and poke the cake with lots of holes using a toothpick.
6. Drizzle 1/2 cup of concentrate over the warm cake.
7. For the icing, mix all ingredients together until smooth, drizzle over cake.

Ingredients:

2 eggs

½ cup butter

½ cup sugar

3 tbsp lemonade concentrate (thawed)

½ cup almond milk

1 ½ cups all purpose flour

1 tsp baking powder

2 tbsp poppy seeds

½ cup lemonade concentrate (thawed)

Icing:

2 Tbsp cream cheese (softened)

1 Tbsp butter, softened

2 Tbsp lemonade concentrate

1 cup powdered sugar

Be Fresh

Bee Tip: Miniaturize this recipe by baking the batter in mini muffin tins. Dip each one half way in icing for cute little lemonade muffin poppers.

HIPPIE BAGELS

with granola & cream cheese

This recipe is a game changer for all bagel and veggie lovers. My silly half bagel, half vegetable combination was inspired by the rainbow bagel creations I stumbled upon in New York. I perfected my own new and natural version using vegetable puree as coloring.

Initially, I only added the veggies for their pigment, but I soon realized after it gave these bagels a very special taste too. A unique flavor of roasted vegetables had harmonized into the fresh and chewy bagel. Nutritious veggies and carbs? Score!

Directions:

1. Mix warm water, yeast, and sugar in a large mixing bowl. Let rest for 5 minutes.
2. Add the vegetable puree to the yeast and slowly stir in the flour. Knead the dough for about 5 minutes.
3. Transfer the dough into a greased bowl and cover. Let rise for about 2 hours, or until doubled in size.
4. Roll out the dough into a snake and then roll it around your hand once to form a circle for the bagel. Cut the end and seal the seam together. (Roll out and layer the different doughs on top of each other, and then cut into stips if using multiple colors.)
5. Let the shaped bagels rise for about 20 minutes.
6. Preheat the oven to 325 degrees.
7. Meanwhile, bring a large pot of water to boil. Add the bagels a few at a time and boil on each side for 1 minute.
8. Brush the bagel with an egg wash (optional) and bake for about 20 minutes, or until light golden in color.
9. Serve with yogurt and your favorite granola.

Ingredients:

1 Tbsp instant yeast

2 Tbsp water

1 tsp sugar or honey

1 cup vegetable/ fruit puree

    -i.e. pureed spinach for

    green, beets for red

2 tsp salt

3-4 cups bread flour

Garnish

cream cheese and

granola

Be Natural

Bee Tip: speaking of unfamiliar flavor combinations, peanut butter and pickles are my all-time favorite camping snack. A perfect topping for Hippie Bagels too!

Snacktime

SOFT PRETZELS

The first time I shared one of my warm, soft pretzels with my friend, Austin, I captured his over the top reaction in a candid photo. Ever since, this recipe makes me feel that ecstatic joy in his smile. A warm, chewy, soft pretzel of mine is known to win to any appetite.

What fascinates me most about pretzel and bagel dough is it's not entirely about the flour, but also about how the dough is boiled. If you haven't tried boiling homemade dough before baking, I highly recommend it. By only using water, you can add a totally new dimension to any dough. For pretzels, baking soda is also added to the water for a pretzel-y taste and dark brown crust.

Directions:

1. Heat milk to about 100 degrees and stir in the yeast and brown sugar. Let rest for about 3-5 minutes.
2. Add the yeast mixture in with the flour, butter, and salt.
3. Using a dough hook or by hand, knead the dough until it comes together into a smooth ball.
4. Place in an oiled bowl, cover, and let rise for 1-2 hour, or doubled in size.
5. Punch down the dough and roll out into a one inch round snake. Twist your pretzels as you please and leave to rise for another 20 minutes.
6. Meanwhile, boil 8 cups of water with baking soda.
7. Dunk each pretzel in the boiling water for about one minutes on each side.
8. Mix together the egg and milk. Brush each pretzel with the egg wash.
9. Bake at 425 for 15-20 minutes, until dark golden brown.

Ingredients:

1 cup milk

1 Tbsp yeast

3 Tbsp brown sugar

2 ¼ cups bread flour

3 Tbsp butter, melted

1 tsp salt

¼ cup baking soda

8 cups of water

Egg Wash

1 egg

2 Tbsp milk

Be Joyful

PORTOBELLO FRIES

with chipotle tahini

As a vegetarian, I have a fond heart for all things mushroom. I try to sneak mushrooms into just about anything and everything. This is my next-level recipe for serving French fries; an excellent umami substitution for russet or sweet potatoes. Plus, Portobello's pack a heck of a lot more flavor and nutrients than potatoes. Frying up these shrooms brings out an umami flavor, my most beloved flavor complex next to sweet, salty, sour, and bitter. It's a naturally occurring, savory flavor in certain foods that's pleasant, bold, and rich. It's quite possibly the 'yum-factor' to these mushrooms that make them simply irresistible.

Directions:

1. Slice portobellos into ½ inch strips and lightly coat in flour.
2. In a small bowl, mix together the parmesan, panko, garlic, and basil.
3. Dip the floured portobellos into the beaten egg and then into the parmesan mixture.
4. Heat a medium sauce pan with a few Tablespoons of olive oil and lightly sear the mushrooms on all sides.
5. For the dipping sauce, blend all ingredients together until smooth.
6. Enjoy!

Ingredients:

4 large Portobello mushrooms

½ cup flour

½ cup finely grated parmesan

½ cup panko

4 cloves minced garlic

1 tsp dried basil

3 eggs, lightly beaten

3 Tbsp olive oil

<u>Chipotle Tahini</u>

¼ cup mayo, or Just Mayo (vegan)

1 Tbsp tahini

1 tsp fresh dill

1 garlic glove, minced

1 chipotle pepper in adobe sauce

Be Confident

Bee Tip: this basic breading technique can be used for lots of vegetables such as eggplant, tomatoes, zucchini and more!

WILD MUSHROOM GUACAMOLE

Sometimes my recipes come from intricately tuning flavors with ingredients, other times they fall into place completely at random. This particular recipe was derived from the forgotten inventory of mushrooms, avocados, and eggs in my fridge. The recipe seemed obvious.

With few ingredients, precision cooking and attention to detail, any stunning dish can be created. This guacamole makes for a perfect spread on a veggie sandwich, a dip for chips, or even soft pretzels (pg. 21)

Directions:

1. In a large sauce pan, heat 2 Tbsp olive oil. Add the mushrooms, season with salt and pepper. Cook for about 20 minutes, stirring occasionally.

2. Meanwhile, in a large bowl mash together the avocado with the remaining ingredients.

3. Fold in the sautéed mushrooms to the guacamole. Serve with your favorite chips or bread.

Bee Tip: To be a little extra random and extravagant, I like to add a soft boiled egg on top. Boil about 6 mins for softer and 12 for harder egg yolks.

Ingredients:

1/2 lb wild mushrooms, chopped

2 Tbsp olive oil

salt and pepper to taste

4 ripe avocados

2 limes, juice and zest

¼ cup cilantro, chopped

1 tsp cumin

2 tsp salt

1 jalapeno, minced

Be Random

RAINBOW CHARD ROLLS
with butternut quinoa filling

As the old proverb goes; you are what you eat. Why not eat vibrant to feel vibrant? A plant's nutrients and colors are the paint to my canvas while cooking. One that always catches my eye at the farmer's markets is rainbow chard.

A quick blanch creates a vibrant, nutrient-dense wrap for just about anything. Not only do these rolls look impressive, they also pack a ton of phytonutrients. As a true plant powerhouse, I promise, rainbow chard will leave you feeling colored with energy.

Directions:

1. Trim the long stems from the chard leaves and blanch the leaves in boiling water for one minute.
2. Immediately tranfser the leaves into an ice bath to chill quickly. Fan out the leaves on a cloth to dry.
3. Meanwhile in a medium saute pan, cook the spinach, peppers, and garlic with a touch of oil until soft and fragrant.
4. Stir in the quinoa, curry powder, and butternut cheez.
5. Scoop 2-3 Tbsp of the quinoa mixture into a blanched leaf and roll it up burrito-style.

Bee Tip: blanched leafy greens are sturdy enough to act as a low carb option for your favorite sandwich wraps.

Ingredients:

6 large rainbow chard leaves

1/2 cup spinach, chopped

1 bell pepper, diced

2 cloves garlic, minced

1/2 cup butternut cheez

(see pg. 57)

2 tsp curry powder

1 cup cooked quinoa

Be
Vibrant

KIMCHI BRUSSELS

with cashew crackers

Perfectly roasting Brussels sprouts is such an impressive way to showcase simplicity with a single ingredient. Once you try one that's light and crispy, a bit salty and sweet, you may never reach to snack on a bag of chips again. Best of all, the medicinal and digestive properties of ginger and brussels sprouts pack a nutritious yet delicious punch.

I invented this recipe as a miniaturized version of The Honey B Cafe's much-loved, Kimchi Bowl. Focusing in on one ingredient can transform one dish into a completely new one. I encourage you to intentionally notice each ingredient you taste in your meals. I assure you it will change the way you cook!

Directions:

1. Preheat the oven to 375 degrees.
2. To make the sesame ginger sauce, puree all ingredient in a blender until smooth.
3. In a large bowl, toss together the brussels sprouts with sesame ginger sauce. Roast for about 30 minutes, until dark golden brown and crispy.
4. To make the crackers, simply pulse all the ingredients in a food processor until smooth.
5. On parchment paper, roll out the cracker dough into a rectangle about ¼ inch thick. Cut the rectangle into 2 inch squares.
6. Bake the crackers at 350 degrees for about 5-7 minutes, until firm and golden brown.
7. Meanwhile, to make the avocado crema, blend all the ingredients on high speed until smooth and creamy.
8. Assemble the crackers with a piece of kimchi, roasted brussels sprouts, and avocado crema.

Ingredients:

1 cup brussels sprouts,
trimmed and halved

2 Tbsp olive oil

salt and pepper, to taste

Sesame Ginger sauce

3 inches ginger, peeled
and chopped

3 cloves garlic

2 Tbsp soy sauce

1/4 cup brown sugar

1/2 cup rice wine vinegar

1/4 cup canola oil

1 tsp sesame oil

Cashew Crackers

1/2 cup cashews

¼ cup sunflower seeds

¼ cup almonds

1 egg

2 cloves garlic

Avocado Crema

1 ripe avocado

¼ cup cilantro

1 lemon, zest and juice

salt and pepper

Bee Tip: Kimchi is a staple food in Korea made from fermented cabbage and spices. It's also a natural probiotic and flavor packed superfood. If you can't find Kimchi, other pickled vegetables work great in this recipe too.

TREE HUGGERS
with ginger peanut sauce

Oh how I love freshly picked asparagus. They're like having little bite sized forests to snack on. I always remember snacking on them when I would visit my friend's farm in Missouri. For this recipe, I tried to captivate my lush spring hiking memories inside a light rice paper wrapper.

I love cooking with rice paper because it's a unique way to incorporate rice. Rather than serving rice as an accompaniment, it can be used as a beautiful iridescent package for your roasted veggies. The *Three Sisters* rice paper wrappers are tactful and thin; perfect for binding your ingredients without an overpowering flavor.

Directions:

1. Toss the asparagus with olive, salt, and lemon pepper.
2. Cook on the grill or in a sauté pan until their vibrant green color pops.
3. To assemble the rolls, soften each rice paper wrapper in a shallow dish with cold water for 1 minute, until soft but still shapely.
4. Lay the wrapper on a flat surface and line with a few leaves of arugula. Pack the roll with a variety of julienned vegetables. Add a small pinch of the cooked rice noodles.
5. Roll up burrito style and refrigerate.
6. To make the peanut sauce, whisk the peanut butter and sesame ginger sauce until creamy.
7. Serve the chilled spring rolls with the dipping sauce.

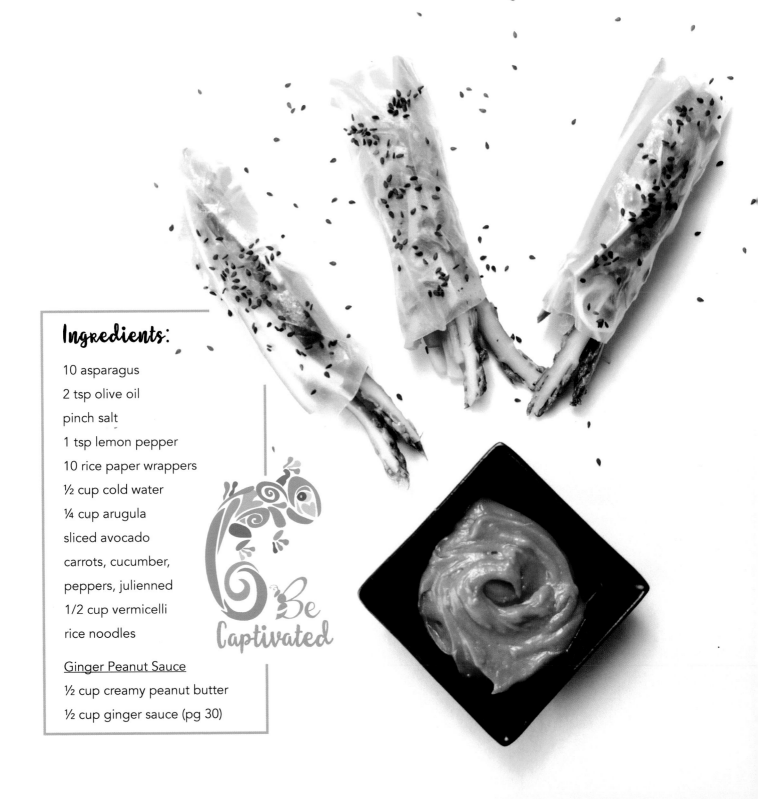

Ingredients:

10 asparagus

2 tsp olive oil

pinch salt

1 tsp lemon pepper

10 rice paper wrappers

½ cup cold water

¼ cup arugula

sliced avocado

carrots, cucumber,

peppers, julienned

1/2 cup vermicelli

rice noodles

Ginger Peanut Sauce

½ cup creamy peanut butter

½ cup ginger sauce (pg 30)

Be Captivated

SCALLOP CEVICHE
with strawberry and avocado

When I first moved to California, I randomly placed myself in a town I never heard of but eventually fell in love with. Sleepy, beachy Ventura, California stole my heart and changed my life. My soul-searching move from freezing Chicago sparked my ambition. I was in awe of the plentiful produce and played with it as a fiery chef was growing inside me.

I lived right across the street from a strawberry field and had an avocado and lemon tree in my very backyard. This was one of the first recipes I created in my California environment. It still tastes like the purest representation of my California self.

Directions:

1. In a small mixing bowl, toss together the scallops with the lemon.
2. Marinate the scallops for about 2 hours until opaque and firm*.
3. Meanwhile, cut the sourdough in ½ inch slices and line on a baking sheet.
4. Drizzle with olive oil and a sprinkle of salt. Bake at 350 for 10-12 minutes, until crispy.
5. To finish the ceviche, toss the marinated scallops with the remaining ingredients.
6. Top the warm toasts with the scallop dip.

Bee Tip: Ceviche involves using acid (like lemon) to denature (or cook) the fish without using heat.

Ingredients:

1 lb bay scallops

3 lemons, juice and zest

2 medium-ripe avocados, cubed

8 ounces strawberries, chopped

¼ cup cilantro, chopped

Be local

CHICKPEA OF THE SEA

in endive cups

I have to admit; the only time I've ever actually made tuna salad was when I was 'forced' to while working at Whole Foods. However, chickpea "tuna" was my game changer. If you didn't tell anyone, I bet 9 times out of 10, they would believe this is the best tuna salad they've ever had. Lightly mashed chickpeas, hidden with a little celery, red onion, packs about the same amount of protein as traditional tuna salad.

Last but not least, Dulse seaweed flakes are the most important component to this fish-like tuna salad. Unlike the seaweed you find your sushi rolled in, fresh Dulse seaweed is like red leaf lettuce. Nutrient dense Dulse gives this salad a near-perfect tuna taste. More power to getting creative with plants while being totally natural.

Directions:

1. Lightly smash the chickpeas in a large bowl and fluff with a fork.
2. In a separate bowl mix the vegan mayo, lemon, salt, dill, and dulse.
3. Stir the mayo mixture into the chickpeas.
4. Fold in the celery and onion.
5. Serve on endive leaves or with your favorite crackers.

Ingredients:

2 (16 oz) cans chickpeas

1/4 cup vegan mayonnaise

1 lemon, juice and zest

2 tsp salt

2 Tbsp fresh dill, minced

2 Tbsp dulse flakes

3 celery stalks, minced

1/2 red onion, minced

Be plant-powered

Bee Tip: Substitute an avocado that's about to turn over-ripe for half of the mayo to make a creamy avocado "tuna" salad with healthier fats.

Gorgeous Greens

TAFFY APPLE SALAD

Oddly, eating marshmallow-whipped cream fluff for Thanksgiving dinner is a yearly tradition in my family, sometimes even for Christmas too. It's been one of those recipes everyone expects to be there for the holidays but I'm not sure anyone genuinely wants. I'm certain it's actually a dessert but we eat it for dinner anyways.

As I sophisticated my culinary works, I was inspired to give this recipe the salad name that it deserves. By removing the copious amounts of whipped cream, this salad turned into a very loose interpretation of the traditional version. Goat cheese, peanuts, apple, and maple dressing create a classic taffy apple taste without overdosing on sugar.

Directions:

1. Toss all ingredients together in a large bowl.
2. To make the dressing, blend the maple, Dijon, vinegar, and salt. Slowly pour in the oil.
3. Toss the ingredients with the dressing. Top with extra peanuts and goat cheese.

Bee Tip: This maple Dijon dressing is a great marinade for cooking fish.
Try brushing your fish with the dressing before cooking and serve it with the taffy apple salad.

Ingredients:

3 medium apples, diced

4 ounces goat cheese, crumbled

½ cup honey roasted peanuts

2 cups spinach

2 cup arugula

2 Tbsp fresh mint, chopped

Maple Dijon Dressing

¼ cup maple syrup

¼ cup olive oil

2 Tbsp Dijon mustard

2 Tbsp apple cider
vinegar

½ tsp salt

Be
Cozy

HONEY B CHOP

After leaving Chicago I realized absence makes the heart grow fonder when it comes to certain foods, like Portillo's. For those unfamiliar, Portillo's is a Chicago food icon serving the best hotdogs, Italian beef, and chopped salads in town. If you mention Portillo's to any Chicagoan outside of Chicago, you've instantly gained a new best friend. It truly shows how the power of food can bring people together.

Sadly my new west coast life had to adapt to life without Portillo's. Their drool-worthy salad chops up a little bit of everything, making each forkful packed and perfectly balanced. I was inspired to spice up their chopped with a bit of my own flare.

Directions:

1. Boil pasta until al dente and crisp the bacon.
2. Toss all of the salad ingredients together in a large bowl.
3. To make the dressing, add all the ingredients together in a blender.
4. Blend on low speed until all ingredients are thoroughly incorporated.
5. Toss the salad with the fresh dressing.
6. Serve with a toasty slice of sourdough.

Bee Tip: The smoked blue cheese in this recipe acts as a vegetarian substitution for the bacon that's usually in Portillos chopped salad. If you're a bacon lover, go ahead and toss some in too.

Ingredients:

½ cup ditalini pasta

1 head romaine, finely chopped

4 ounces cherry tomatoes, halved

1 cucumber, diced

1 small red onion, diced

2 ounce smoked blue cheese

Creamy Italian Dressing

¼ cup mayonnaise

2 lemons, juice and zest

2 Tbsp cup olive oil

4 cloves garlic

¼ cup fresh basil

1 tsp oregano

3 Tbsp parmesan

Be
balanced

LIL' MISS CRISP

I'm all about twisting ingredients upside down to reinvent their appearance and put emphasis on their flavor. This recipe unfolded as a very loose interpretation of a Caesar salad. The delicate crisped parmesan tuiles serve as a replacement for the shaved parmesan and croutons. The fat, juicy heirloom tomatoes and farmers market romaine cradle the cheese crisp 'gold mines' in this salad. A medley so thoughtful yet simple.

Instead of tossing a bunch of misfit veggies in a bowl for another bland salad, I like to experience each of the ingredients individually. It really makes the meal so much more pleasant.

Directions:

1. Preheat the oven to 350 degrees.
2. To make the parmesan tuiles, shape the shaved parmesan into a 1 inch pile on a parchment line baking sheet.
3. Bake the cheese for 2-3 minutes until golden. While the cheese is still hot, bend each circle of parmesan into a U shape until hardened.
4. To make the dressing, simply blend all the ingredients together until smooth.
5. Toss the romaine, tomatoes, shaved parmesan, and dressing. Top with the parmesan crisps.

Ingredients:

4 ounces grated parmesan

1 head crisp romaine leaves

4-5 local heirloom tomatoes

shaved parmesan

<u>Creamy Lemon Dressing</u>

¼ cup mayonnaise

3 lemons, juice and zest

2 Tbsp cup olive oil

4 cloves garlic

3 Tbsp parmesan

salt and pepper, to taste

Be centered

Bee Tip: These pretty little tuiles can be made out of a variety of different hard cheeses such as Asiago or Romano.

CALIFORNIA DREAMIN'

Before moving out to California, I never thought my winters would involve plump pomegranates casually growing outside my window where sparkling icicles used to grow. I created this recipe during my last California winter, as an appreciation for the year-round bounty of produce here. After living out in sunshine for years, you tend to forget that beautiful crops don't just flourish anywhere.

While I was mindlessly gathering brussel sprouts and avocados, soaking in the sun at the farmer's market, I remembered there was actually blistering winds and three feet of snow back home. How fortunate I am to have such produce privileges. With that being said, try to notice what's flourishing around you for sustainable cooking. For me, pomegranate is like breaking open a gemstone, a necessity to make this winter salad burst with flavor.

Directions:

1. Simmer the quinoa in 1 cup of water until all the water is absorbed.
2. To make the dressing, blend all ingredients together except oil and poppy seeds. Slowly drizzle in the oil. Stir in the poppy seeds.
3. Toss the quinoa and dressing with the remaining ingredients.

Ingredients:

½ cup quinoa

1 cup shaved brussels sprouts

1 cup shredded kale

¼ cup shaved almonds

¼ cup hemp seeds

1 pomegrante, seeded

Be mindful

Lemon Poppy Seed Dressing

2 lemons, juice and zest

1/4 cup apple cider vinegar

½ yellow onion, chopped

¼ cup sugar

2 tsp Dijon mustard

1 tsp salt

¼ cup olive oil

Bee Tip: Hemp seeds, quinoa, and almonds are all great ways to sneak in some plant-powered protein

BEAUTY & THE BALSAMIC

In California, I discovered avocados and butter are interchangable. They're also used for breakfast, lunch, and dinner. Avocados are indefinitely essential to a California lifestyle. When I made the leap over here, I started adding it in everything; Salads, soups, sauces, smoothies and desserts! When they are so plentiful, it just seems natural.

The avocado in this dressing is ever so slightly masked by a sweet balsamic dressing, while still making your taste buds question what exactly that buttery flavor is. Be sure to wait until your avocados are perfectly ripe, so they can whip up smoothly with the silky honey and balsamic.

Directions:

1. Preheat the oven to 375 degrees.
2. Toss the diced beets in olive oil, salt, and pepper and spread on a parchment lined baking sheet.
3. Roast for about 30 min, until softened and caramelized.
4. For the dressing, blend all ingredients together until smooth.
5. Toss the cooked beets with the dressing and remaining salad ingredients.

Ingredients:

3-4 medium beets, peeled and diced

1 Tbsp olive oil

salt and pepper

1 cup shredded kale

½ red onion, thinly sliced

¼ cup hemp seeds

¼ pine nuts

Avocado Balsamic

1/2 cup balsamic dressing

½ cup honey

1 ripe avocado

2 Tbsp olive oil

1 tsp salt

Be Grateful

Bee Tip: You can add an extra avocado in this dressing to make it into a fabulous and unique sandwich spread.

PUMPKIN BRUSSELS

Fall is one of my favorite times of year because more than any season, you can taste fall's flavors simply by the feeling in the air. Noticing how flavors taste in the culinary world is an important but small part of the equation. Creating a recipe touches all of your senses and can spark even your deepest emotions.

The spice of cinnamon, when combined with ginger, nutmeg, allspice, and clove, turns into an entire season. Pumpkin pie spice reigns over all the food, drink, candles, and soaps in the Fall because of how nice and cozy it makes us feel. This recipe hits the spot at The Honey B during Santa Barbara's fall, when the weather hasn't quite cooled down yet. A cozy pumpkin spice flavor while still having a cool crisp salad.

Directions:

1. Preheat your oven the 375 degrees.
2. Toss together the sweet potatoes, olive oil, and spices.
3. Spread the sweet potatoes on a parchment lined baking sheet and cook for about 30 minutes, until soften and golden.
4. To make the dressing, blend all the ingredients together except oil. Slowly whisk in the oil until incorporated.
5. In a large bowl, toss the remaining salad ingredients together with the dressing.

Bee Tip: Any type of winter squash can be a nice substitute for roasted sweet potatoes in this recipe.

Ingredients:

1 large sweet potato, diced

2 Tbsp olive oil

1 tsp pumpkin spice

1 tsp salt

1 cup brussels sprouts, shaved

1 cup shredded kale

¼ cup dried cranberries

½ red onion, thinly sliced

½ cup roasted pumpkin seeds

Pumpkin Spice Dressing

½ cup apple cider vinegar

2-3 Tbsp honey

2 tsp pumpkin spice

1 tsp cinnamon

1 tsp salt

¼ cup olive oil

Queen bee Dinners

GARLIC SALMON

with shiitakes & green tea noodles

Possibly my favorite party pleasing recipe. The rich blend of shiitakes, garlic, and salmon almost makes me want to cry out of pure happiness. My favorite flavor combo also happens to be my three most adored ingredients. Every time I'm making salmon, I find shiitakes and garlic somehow sneaking in.

Nearly every ingredient in this recipe is a top superfood. Garlic and turmeric combating sickness, shiitakes fighting obesity, and the omega-3s in salmon strengthening the brain; all teaming up to create a superfood army. An incredibly comforting dish leaving you with an abundance of energy.

Directions:

1. In a large pan, saute half the garlic and ginger with 2 Tbsp butter until fragrant. Toss in the cilantro.
2. Scoop the garlic mixture on top of the salmon and bring another Tbsp of butter to high heat. Sear the salmon on each side for about 2 minutes. While cooking, season with salt and pepper and glaze with the garlic mixture.
3. Remove from the heat and cover the salmon with a lid to finish off cooking. The salmon will slowly steam and cook through in about 5 minutes.
4. Meanwhile, in a sauce pan, cook the shiitakes and bell peppers in the remainder of butter with rest of the garlic and ginger until lightly soft and golden brown.
5. Cook the green tea noodles according to instructions. Toss the mushrooms, peppers and noodles together. *if you can't find pre-made green tea noodles in a grocery store, you can boil soba noodles in green tea instead of water. Serve the seared salmon with the tossed noodles.

Ingredients:

- 1 lb salmon
- ½ cup butter
- ¼ cup minced ginger
- 8-10 cloves of garlic
- 3 Tbsp cilantro, minced
- 1 lb shiitake mushrooms
- 3 red bell peppers, julienne
- 2 cups green tea noodles

Be strong

Bee Tip: Buy healthy and sustainable fish by educating yourself on the source of your fish. Instead of Salmon, try checking out what's fresh and local.

UNIVERSAL CURRY

with seasonal veggies

Simple to make, complex in flavors, and guaranteed to enhance just about any dish. This thick and creamy curry sauce never fails to impress and the best part is, it's incredibly healthy. Packed with turmeric, a fierce and powerful spice both tastefully and medicinally, its healing properties can fight and even reverse diseases. Have you noticed yet? I'm nuts for coconuts! Immunity boosting, energizing, and hydrating, among many other benefits, coconuts were sure born with some crazy super powers. Using coconut cream in this recipe results in a creamier recipe and denser amount of fats and nutrients, so a little goes a long way!

Directions:

1. Preheat your oven to 350 degrees.
2. In a sauce pan, bring all the sauce ingredients together to a simmer, whisking until thoroughly combined.
3. Toss your favorite seasonal veggies together with a little olive oil, salt, and pepper. Roast to your desire.
4. Pour the warm curry sauce over your veggies with a bed of brown rice, chickpeas, etc.

Bee Tip: When serving rice with curry, I like to pre-infuse my rice by cooking it with ½ coconut cream and ½ water. Makes for a rich, decadent curry bowl.

Ingredients:

<u>Sauce</u>

2 cans coconut cream

3 Tbsp your favorite curry powder

2 Tbsp tumeric

4-5 cloves minced garlic

1/4 cup honey

2 Tbsp soy sauce

<u>Accompaniments</u>

Your favorite roasted veggies:

Brown rice

chickpeas

cucumber

avocado

chives

Be fierce

BUTTERNUT MAC n' CHEEZ

If my stomach could tolerate it, cheese would definitely be my main food group. It's one of the most difficult ingredients to accurately substitute being lactose intolerant or vegan. I attempted to like the mass-produced vegan cheese at grocery stores, but I knew there had to be another wholesome way to do it. After many trials and errors, I can happily share my favorite version of a nut-free, plant-based cheese. Pureed roasted butternut squash and coconut cream dance together beautifully for a completely natural velveeta style cheez sauce.

Directions:

1. Preheat the oven to 375 degrees.

2. Toss diced butternut squash with olive oil and salt and pepper.

3. Spread evenly on a baking tray and roasted for about 20 minutes, until lightly browned.

4. Meanwhile, boil the macaroni noodles.

5. When the squash is done, transfer it to a blender with the coconut cream, butter, garlic, salt, and pepper.

6. Toss the creamy sauce with the cooked macaroni noodles.

7. Transfer the mac n cheese into an oven-safe serving dish. Top the mac n cheese with panko or potato chips (my family's favorite) and bake for another 5-10 min to brown the crust.

Ingredients:

1 large butternut squash,
peeled and diced

2 Tbsp olive oil

salt and pepper, to taste

1 lb macaroni noodles

¼ cup coconut cream

¼ cup vegan butter (such as
Earth Balance)

4-5 cloves garlic

2 tsp salt

2 tsp pepper

1/4 cup panko

<u>Garnish</u>

cilantro

Be wholesome

TAHINI PEPPER SOUP

Often times, I will casually meander around the grocery store or farmer's market, and almost let a recipe create itself based on what ingredients catch my eye. For this recipe, I came across the most beautiful mixed peppers at the farmer's market and soon after spotted an affordable organic tahini paste. A little lemon zest, and I knew this was a soup match made in heaven.

Tahini, aka ground sesame seeds, is a key component commonly hiding in hummus. It's also one of my favorite 'secret ingredients' to hide in other recipes. Tahini compliments both savory and sweet, adding a rich uniqueness to recipes.

Directions:

1. Heat the oven to broil. Toss the peppers and tomatoes in olive oil, salt, and pepper.
2. Spread the veggies on a parchment lined baking sheet and broil until partially blackened.
3. Peel off charred skin if desired and puree in a blender or food processor until smooth.
4. Slowly add in the stock, tahini, lemon, herbs and spices.
5. Serve the soup hot or cold with an extra swirl of tahini.

Bee Tip: To turn this soup into a well rounded meal, add a scoop of cooked quinoa, roasted veggies, or your favorite beans

Ingredients:

10 bell peppers

3 lbs very ripe tomatoes

2 Tbsp olive oil

salt and pepper, to taste

1 cup vegetable stock

½ cup tahini paste

1 lemon, juice and zest

1 tsp cayenne pepper

1 tsp coriander

¼ cup fresh basil

¼ cup cilantro

Be observant

BLACK BEAN SLIDERS

Living in Chicago, right across from Sultan's Market, I fell in love with falafel. I worked Sultan's falafel into my diet multiple times a week. Who can resist affordable, genuine flavors that fill you up and keep you happy the rest of the day. Now that's what I call a winning recipe. While I was trying to recreate Sultan's falafel, I started to notice all the flavor possibilities making falafel. I decided to replace chickpeas for black beans, still keeping it silly affordable. I added some walnuts for richness, quinoa for texture, and realized I was creating an entirely new masterpiece. Since I was working on this creation at my café, without a fryer, stove, or oven, I pressed this black bean creation on the waffle iron. Wala! A perfectly textured, compact little veggie slider, filled with protein and an eerie resemblance to true sliders.

Directions:

1. Soak black beans in cold water overnight to soften, or boil the beans for one minute and let rest for 1-2 hours.
2. To make the barebecue sauce, simmer all ingredients in a sauce pan until reduced to half. Using an immersion blender or transfer to a stand blender and puree until smooth.
3. Drain the black beans and pulse in a food processor with the remaining ingredients except quinoa until the mixture is finely ground and malleable. Stir in the cooked quinoa.
4. Heat your waffle iron and shape the black bean mixture into 1 inch circles.
5. On a well-oiled surface, press each patty in the waffle iron for 2-3 minutes, until browned and crispy.
6. Serve the patties on slider buns with lettuce, tomato, pickles, red onion, and blueberry barbecue.

Ingredients:

Black bean sliders

1 cup dried black beans

1/2 yellow onion, chopped

1/2 cup walnuts

¼ cup fresh parsley

¼ cup cilantro

5 cloves garlic

2 tcp cumin

1 tsp coriander

2 tsp salt

1/2 cup blueberry
barbecue sauce

1/2 cup cooked quinoa

Blueberry Barbecue

1 cup fresh blueberries

1/4 cup brown sugar

1/4 cup balsamic vinegar

4 cloves garlic, minced

1 yellow onion, minced

3 Tbsp chipotle peppers

2 Tbsp cumin

1 Tbsp ground coffee

1 dark beer

salt, pepper to taste

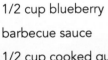

Be versatile

JACKFRUIT SOULBREAD

I've had multiple friends leery of jackfruit due to its genuinely meaty taste, texture, and appearance. It's texture is similar to pulled pork. However, it's actually a very large fruit from Asia that's finding a new purpose as a meaty plant-based substitute in the vegan community.

Cooking jackfruit, I discovered rice cookers can be used for so much more than making rice. In this case, as jackfruit slow cooks, it pulls into stringy pieces resembling pulled pork. Like magic, the jackfruit acts like a sponge as it cooks with different herbs and spices, transforming its flavor entirely after slow cooking.

Directions:

1. Pour all jackfruit ingredients into the rice cooker. Let cook for a cycle of rice.

2. Meanwhile, blend all crema ingredients until smooth.

3. To make the cornbread waffles, stir together the melted vegan butter and coconut milk. Slowly stir in the remainder of the ingredients until thoroughly incorporated.

4. Press the cornbread batter on your greased waffle iron for 3-4 minutes, until golden and crispy.

5. To assemble the dish, blend all the chipotle-sauce ingredients together until smooth and pour over the slow cooked jackfruit. Using a fork or your hands, mash apart the jackfruit until it looks like the texture of pulled pork.

6. Top the warm cornbread waffles with jackfruit, arugula, red onions, black beans, and cilantro.

Ingredients:

Jackfruit

3 cans jackfruit in brine

6 cups of water

1 can coconut cream

2-3 chipotles in adobe

6 cloves minced garlic

1/4 c brown sugar

2 tsp salt

Chipotle Sauce

1 can coconut milk

2 chipotle chilies in adobe

3 cloves garlic

3 Tbsp brown sugar

2 tsp salt

Cornbread Waffles

2 cup coconut milk

1/2 cup vegan butter

(Earth Balance)

½ cup roasted corn

2 cups cornmeal

2 tsp ground flaxseed

2 tsp baking powder

2 tsp salt

¼ cup fresh chives, chopped

Avocado crema

1 ripe avocado

¼ cup cilantro

1 lemon, zest + juice

salt and pepper

Garnish

arugula, red onion,

black beans,

avocado

Be adaptable

THAI CURRY PIZZA

After my trip to Thailand, I was head-over-heels in love with Thai culture and cuisine. Upon my return, I meticulously browsed Asian markets and even made friends with a local Thai family living in Missouri. I discovered my best recipes often bloom from a collision of ideas I'm fascinated with. Having been a pizza-obsessed student, I can happily admit the thickened green curry sauce and fabulous Thai toppings to be the best pizza combo of all time.

Directions:

1. Mix honey, water, and yeast in a stand mixer or large bowl and let sit for 5 minutes.
2. Add the salt and olive. Slowly incorporate the flour until the dough starts to pull together. Knead in just enough flour for it not to stick to your hands.
3. Place dough in a bowl lightly coated with olive oil. Cover with plastic wrap or a towel.
4. Let rise for about 2 hours, or until doubled in size.
5. Meanwhile, heat your grill and prep the topping for the pizza.
6. In a medium sauce pan, toast the garlic, and ginger with a bit of olive oil, salt and pepper.
7. Add the coconut cream and fish sauce. Simmer until reduced to half. Stir in the honey.
8. When the dough is doubled, punch down the dough and roll it into a rustic circle.
9. Lay the rolled dough directly on the heated grill. Let crisp up until it has nicely colored grill marks.
10. Flip the dough over and begin to assemble your pizza with the sauce and toppings.
11. Once the dough is cooked through, remove from the heat and garnish with fresh cilantro and peanuts.

Ingredients:

Pizza dough

4 cups bread flour

2 tsp salt

1 tsp honey

2 1/2 tsp instant dry yeast

1 1/2 cups water, 110 degrees

2 Tbsp olive oil

Thai Curry

3-4 cloves garlic

1 Tbsp fish sauce

1 inch ginger, minced

2 cans coconut cream

3-4 Tbsp green curry paste

2 Tbsp honey

salt and pepper, to taste

Toppings

shredded carrot

bean sprouts

cooked shrimp

Garnish

cilantro

crushed peanuts

Be fascinated

RAINBOW LASAGNA

A breath-taking recipe I created in Chicago in hopes of getting out of a job rut. I designed this recipe for an audition to be on The Food Network, ironically, a year prior to winning a different cooking show. I put everything on the line to make these shine, dance, and sing for the judges. While it may have not been what they were looking for, it was just what I needed to feel inspired again.

Like a kid in a candy store, I gravitate towards all the pretty colors compiled in our produce. I can't help but to go into a grocery store and imagine all the fruits and veggies as paints in an art store. Try cooking up your own colorful expression!

Directions:

1. Season the sliced vegetables with a little olive oil, salt, and pepper. Cook on an outdoor grill or grill pan until nice char marks form.
2. To make the tomato sauce layer, puree the sundried tomatoes, basil, and fresh tomatoes together.
3. To make the cashew ricotta, soak the cashews overnight in water or soak for one hour in boiling water to soften.
4. Puree the soaked cashews with the remaining ingredients. Set aside.
5. Mix together the butternut cheez with the cooked quinoa.
6. To assemble, lay the grilled zuchhini on the bottom of a 9 inch baking dish. Top with a layer of cashew ricotta. Lay the yellow squash on top followed by a layer of the butternut mixture. Place the grilled eggplant for the next layer and top with the tomato sauce.
7. Serve warm or cold garnished with fresh basil.

Bee Tip: To play around with texture, try making this recipe completely raw. Thinly slice raw veggies such as beets, carrots, and asaparagus in the layers.

Ingredients:

1 eggplant, sliced ¼ inch thick

1 yellow squash, sliced ¼ inch thick

1 zuchinni, sliced ¼ inch thick

¼ cup sundried tomatoes

¼ cup fresh basil

½ cup diced tomatoes

Cashew Ricotta

½ cup cashews

3-4 cloves garlic

1 lemon, juice and zest

2 tsp salt

2 tsp olive oil

2 tsp nutritional yeast

¼ cup fresh basil

Butternut cheese (pg.57)

½ up cooked quinoa

Garnish

fresh basil

Be dynamic

PISTACHIO POT STICKERS

If I had to choose, pistachios would be the king of the nuts. They even have a perfect double hinged doorway to heaven. Monys, my all-time favorite taco spot in Santa Barbara, has avocado and pistachio salsas up for grabs at their shop. All my dreams come true, in a nutshell.This recipe is a cross between a Mony's-style pistachio salsa and my favorite pistachio pesto. I used the sauce to accompany a hand-pressed potsticker instead of a taco. Similar to a wheat-based spring roll wrapper, Gyoza wrappers create an easy dumpling with a few quick folds. Sautéing them in a few teaspoons of oil is a healthy way to make this recipe nice and crispy.

Directions:

1. Unfold one goyza wrapper and fill it with a dollop of avocado, tomato jam, and cheese on half of the wrapper.
2. Fold the other half over the top and secure the edges by curling them in.
3. Repeat with remaining ingredients.
4. Heat a large saute pan with 2 Tbsp oil and cook the pot stickers on each side for 3-5 minutes, until crisp and golden brown.
5. To make the salsa, pulse all the ingredients in a food processor until almost smooth.
6. Serve the warm pot stickers with the salsa.

Ingredients:

10 gyoza wrappers

2 ripe avocados, mashed

¼ cup minced sundried tomatoes or Red Hen Cannary spicy tomato jam

¼ cup your favorite blue cheese

2 Tbsp olive oil

Pistachio Basil Salsa

1/2 cup shelled pistachios

1 shallot, minced

2 cloves garlic

2 lemons, juiced and zest

2 Tbsp olive oil

¼ cup freh basil

¼ cup fresh parsley

2 Tbsp fresh mint

Garnish

fresh cilantro

Be nutty

Bee Tip: These fool-proof pot stickers can be filled with endless combinations. I'll leave it up to your imagination!

Sweet as Honey

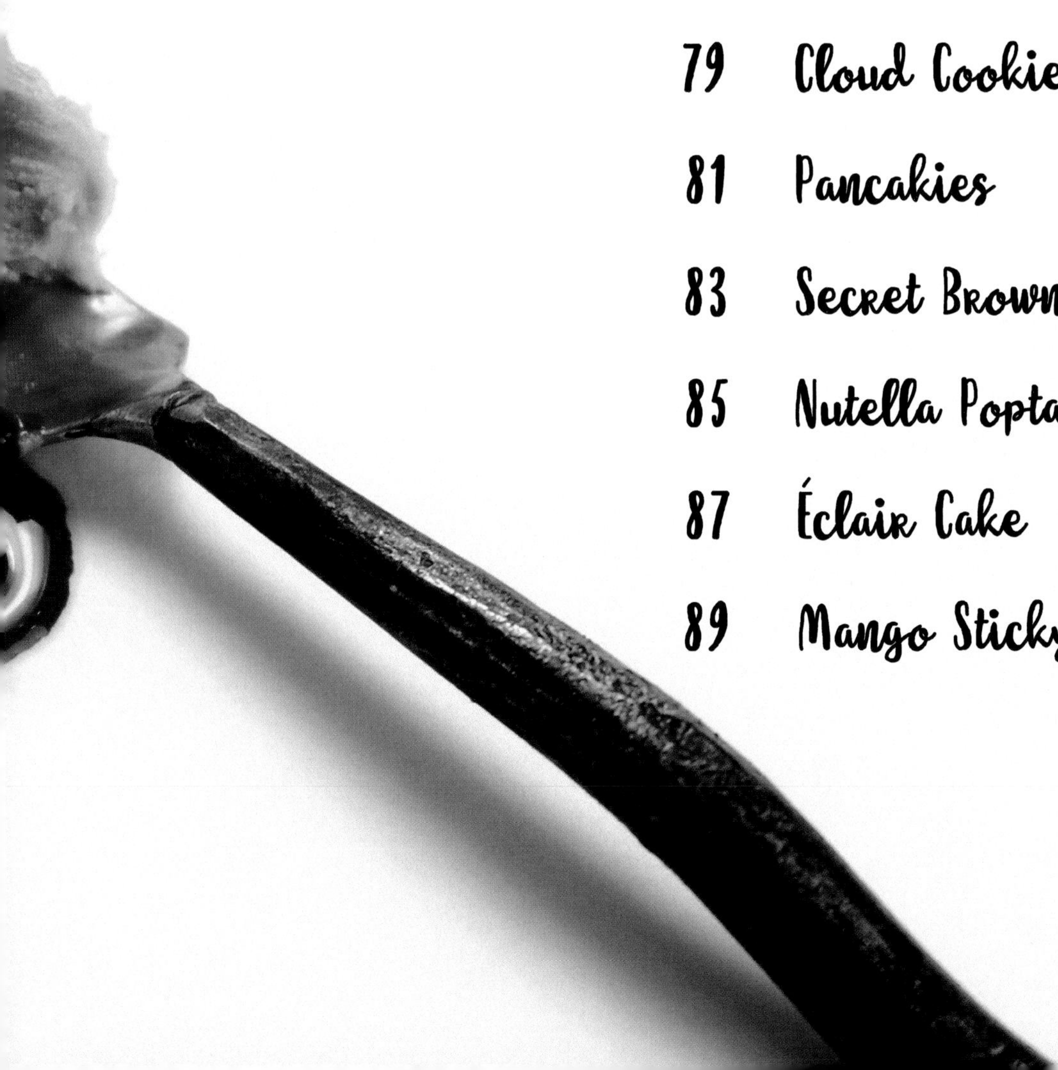

KOLACHES

Kolaches, also known as "doody cookies" in my family, hold a very special place in my heart. I can easily confess, this is hands down my favorite cookie recipe. A few simple ingredients mixed with a little bit of love makes the very best cookie for sharing. Traditionally, we make apricot, raspberry, and prune; but the possibilities are endless when it comes to filling for these little guys.

I like to make Kolaches in mass quantities for the holidays to give away and share with family and friends. The dough takes less than five minutes to make and can be refrigerated for a week. I think everyone can find a little time to share some love, and bake Kolaches. Have a cookie, enjoy the simple things in life.

Directions:

1. In a stand mixer, cream together the butter, cream cheese, and cream.
2. Add the flour and mix until combined.
3. Cover and refrigerate the dough at least 2 hours, or overnight.
4. Preheat the oven to 350 degrees.
5. Heavily dust a clean surface with powdered sugar. Roll out the dough, using the sugar to prevent sticking, 1/2 inch thick.
6. Shape the cookies with a flower or circle cookie cutter. Press your thumb into each cookie and top it with a small dollop of jam.
7. Bake for 6-10 minutes, until puffy and lightly golden.

Ingredients:

2 cups flour

1 cup butter, softened

8 ounces cream cheese,
softened

2 Tbsp cream

powdered sugar

your favorite jam

Be Simple

Bee Tip: Powdered sugar can easily be substituted instead of flour to roll other types of cookies too.
It will prevent dough from becoming too dry and adds a bit more sweetness.

RED VELVET CHEESECAKES

In all honesty, I believe my vegan cheesecake recipe is better than my actual cheesecake recipe. That's saying a lot, having my actual cheesecake recipe win a TV show. I promise, this plant-based cheesecake will knock your socks off. As a devoted cheesecake lover, these cheesecakes are truly magical.

The silky base of this cashew-blend cheesecake can be used to make endless cheesecake flavors. Maybe try stirring in some peanut butter, mixed berries, or both! I have created over twenty different flavors of cheesecake with this ever so simple base batter. The next vegan-style Cheesecake Factory concept perhaps?

Directions:

1. Add all ingredients to a blender except cocoa and beet juice. Puree until silky smooth.

2. Reserve ¼ of the vanilla cashew batter.

3. Puree the cocoa powder and beet juice into the remaining batter.

4. Pour the red velvet batter into lined mini muffin tins. Chill for about 30 min to harden.

5. Pour a thin layer of the reserved vanilla batter on top of the chilled red velvet cheesecakes.

6. Chill the mini cheesecakes for about 3 hours or overnight, until completely hardened.

Ingredients:

3 cups cashews, soaked in
water overnight
1 cup coconut cream
1/2 cup coconut oil
1/2 lemon juice, and zest
1/2 tsp salt
1 cup organic powdered sugar
1/2 cup cocoa powder
2 Tbsp beet juice

Be lovely

Bee Tip: to change the flavor, simply substitute the cocoa and beet with
your favorite goodies such a fruit purees, caramel, or chocolate (see pg. 71)

BANANA BREAD
WAFFLES

A winning combination of gooey chocolate morsels melting into light and fluffy banana bread. This was the second recipe I ever learned to perfect; after Kolaches. As a kid, I would hide our bananas in a brown bag so no one would eat them, and I would *have* to use the over ripe ones for banana bread. This recipe makes two large loaves that last approximately 10 minutes after they're pulled out of the oven, at least in my home. I knew this recipe had to be a part of my café, but we had the fun challenge of working without an oven. Sometimes having obstacles can be the creator of your greatest successes. Subsequently, our waffle iron turned into our oven. We try to waffle just about anything! I had leftover banana bread batter one day and tossed it into our iron. An innovative crisp, dimpled version of my favorite banana bread.

Directions:

1. In a stand mixer, beat together the oil and sugar. Slowly add in each egg.
2. Stir in the flour, baking powder, soda, vanilla, and salt.
3. Alternatively, mix in the mashed banana and buttermilk.
4. Fold in the mini chocolate chips and walnuts, if desired.
5. Press the batter in your waffle iron for 3-4 minutes, until golden brown.

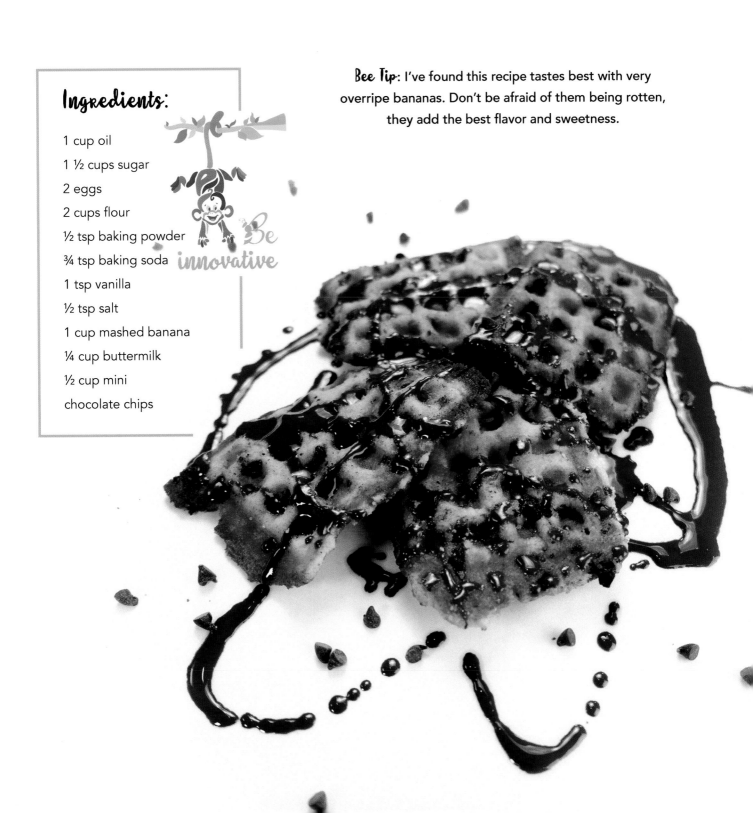

Ingredients:

1 cup oil

1 ½ cups sugar

2 eggs

2 cups flour

½ tsp baking powder

¾ tsp baking soda

1 tsp vanilla

½ tsp salt

1 cup mashed banana

¼ cup buttermilk

½ cup mini
chocolate chips

Bee Tip: I've found this recipe tastes best with very overripe bananas. Don't be afraid of them being rotten, they add the best flavor and sweetness.

Be
innovative

CLOUD COOKIES
with whipped honey

Growing up with a healthy dose of triple berry pie, kolaches, and banana bread, I've always saved room for desserts. I distinctly remember drooling over those big, puffy sugar cookies at the grocery store with a schmear of frosting a mile high.

I was always the weird kid who would scrape the frosting glob off my cupcakes and cookies; so my style of these cookies are simplified with whipped honey on top. I discovered San Marcos Farms local whipped honey creation at the Ojai farmers market. A beautiful honey spun and aerated like cotton candy wisps, mixed with zesty lemon. You match the satisfaction of fluffy frosting without all the added sugar.

Directions:

1. Preheat the oven to 350 degrees. Cream together the sugar and butter.
2. Add the eggs, sour cream, and vanilla.
3. Slowly incorporate the flour, baking powder and salt.
4. Shape the dough into 2 inch circles. Line on a parchment lined baking sheet.
5. Bake for 7-10 minutes until very lightly browned.
6. Top the cookies with a schmear of whipped honey.

Ingredients:

1 cup sugar

½ cup butter, softened

2 eggs

½ cup sour cream

1 tsp fresh vanilla bean

2 cups flour

2 tsp baking powder

½ tsp salt

whipped honey

Be
Sweet

PANCAKIES

Part sugar cookie, part pancake, a Pancakie is a skillet-flipped cookie hybrid. This particular cookie recipe when cooked on a skillet, gets browned and buttery like a pancake. The skillet cooking method gives pancakies a unique coloring, as if it's secretly trying to be a pancake.

Baking cookies on a stovetop turned out to be my perfect solution to fulfill my warm cookie craving without turning on the oven. Making warm, fresh cookies has almost been made too easy. It made me slightly question; why cookies aren't acceptable to eat for breakfast if pancakes are? Same process, different dough. I'll put this one in the dessert section, just in case.

Directions:

1. Beat together the butter, shortening, and sugar until fluffy and pale yellow.
2. Add the egg and vanilla.
3. Slowly mix in the flour and baking powder until incorporated.
4. Chill dough at least 2 hours, or overnight.
5. Heat an oiled skillet on medium high heat. Roll out the cookie dough into a 1 inch circles. Flatten the dough onto the skillet and cook for 2-3 minutes on each side.
6. Serve with a little something sweet.

Ingredients:

½ cup butter

½ cup shortening

1 cup sugar

1 egg

1 tsp vanilla bean

2 ¼ cups flour

1/4 tsp baking

powder

<u>Garnish</u>

honey and toasted

coconut

SECRET BROWNIES

For the most part, I am a believer of "everything in moderation." I don't like to mess with a rich recipe to make it healthy, unless you absolutely positively perfect it. Happily, I can admit this to be a perfectly approved counterpart for my ultra-fudgy brownies. Black beans and avocado in brownies may sound scary, but don't think too much about it. Adding beans to the brownie mix lowers the fat content but still leaves the creaminess, and gives this recipe a boost in protein. The avocado subs for a healthy fat, and gives you another reason to eat more avocados. On top of that, this recipe is completely gluten free! Go ahead, cut yourself a little bit bigger slice, I won't tell anyone!

Directions:

1. Preheat your oven to 350 degrees.
2. In a food processor, puree the black beans, eggs, and avocado.
3. Transfer the mixture into a large bowl and stir in the remaining ingredients.
4. Pour the batter into a greased 9 inch baking dish. Bake for about 20 minutes, until the center is set.
5. To make the frosting, mix all ingredients together until smooth.

Ingredients:

1 (15 oz) can black beans, drained and rinsed

2 eggs

1 ripe avocado

1 Tbsp coconut oil

½ cup cocoa powder

½ tsp baking powder

¼ tsp baking soda

1 tsp vanilla beans

½ cup brown sugar

½ cup dark chocolate chips

Frosting:

1 cup powdered sugar

1/4 cup cocoa powder

2 Tbsp vegan butter, melted

2 Tbsp almond milk

Be Sophisticated

NUTELLA POPTARTS

with orange whiskey marmalade

Mix a rich ribbon of Nutella in a buttery crust and I'm pretty sure that's what heaven tastes like. Wait to play around with this bold recipe for special occasions; like when you feel like treating yourself to pie, cake, and maybe cookies and ice cream too. This pop tart came from a cookie/pie hybrid idea. It might be worth a try to customize your favorite cookie dough with your favorite pastry or pie filling. Certainly, this recipe would not be as adored without the mastery of orange Whiskey jam from Red Hen Canary. I feel so fortunate to live in a town with such beautiful artisans to collaborate with. You should too!

Directions:

1. Mix together the flour, sugars, and butter in a food processor or cut with two knives into pea sized crumbles.
2. Add the coconut oil and pulse to incorporate.
3. Slowly pour in the ice water until the dough starts to pull together.
4. Cover the dough tightly and refrigerate overnight.
5. Roll out the chilled dough 1/4 inch think. Using a cookie cutter, cut out 3X5 inch rectangles of dough.
6. Spread a layer of Nutella on the rectangle, leaving a 1/4 inch border. Top with jam.
7. Place another rectangle of dough on top and seal the edges with a fork.
8. Brush lightly with egg beaten with a little bit of water.
9. Bake for 15-20 minutes, until light golden brown.
10. For the icing, mix ingredients together until smooth. Add a little more / less milk for desired consistency.
11. Chill the baked tarts in the fridge. Top with a drizzle of icing.

Ingredients:

2 cups flour

¼ cup brown sugar

¼ cup granulated sugar

¾ cup butter, cold, diced

¼ cup coconut oil

4-5 Tbsp ice cold water

1 cup orange whiskey jam

1 cup nutella

egg wash

Icing

1 cup powdered sugar

2 Tbsp cream cheese

2 Tbsp butter, softened

1 orange, zest and juice

2 tsp milk

1 tsp vanilla

¼ tsp salt

Bee Tip: Try using this poptart recipe to create a variety of flavors savory or sweet. Apple and brie tucked inside works beautifully!

Be Collaborative

ÉCLAIR CAKE

I'm not sure it's even fair to call this a cake, but that's what I first heard it identified as. It's more like a cake's cool cousin. The graham crackers marry with the whippy mix overnight and transform into a light and creamy no-bake cake. I loved making this cake for summer birthdays in Chicago when it was too hot out to turn on the oven. It's also a great cake recipe for ones who claim they "don't like cake." Truly, I will always find a way to share and eat cake.

I first was served a homemade slice of eclair cake while doing relief work for Hurricane Katrina. I immediately had to ask for the recipe and was so surprised it was mostly whipped cream and graham crackers. My version has a little more chocolate, naturally.

Directions:

1. Whisk the vanilla pudding and milk together until think. Gently fold in the whipped topping.
2. For the frosting, blend together all ingredients until smooth.
3. Line the bottom of a 13 X 9 pan with graham crackers covering the entire bottom.
4. Spread half of the whipped cream mixture on top of the graham crackers.
   Top with half of the chocolate frosting.
5. Repeat another layer of graham crackers, cream, and frosting.
6. Refrigerate overnight.

Ingredients:

1 lb graham crackers

6 ½ ounce instant vanilla pudding

3 cups milk

8 oz frozen whipped cream

Frosting

3 cups powdered sugar

1 cup cocoa powder

6 Tbsp butter, softened

2/3 cup milk

1 Tbsp corn syrup

2 tsp vanilla

Be cool

MANGO STICKY DONUTS

With a little immagination, you can find endless freedom while cooking. If you think about it, you can eat just about anything if you learn to create it. Instead of resorting to the same five or six foods every day, try taking small adventures with your recipes.

I love studying other chef's imaginations to help inspire my own. I recently discovered sushi donuts in LA, which provoked me to create one of my own favorite rice dishes, kao neo mamuong, or Mango Sticky Rice. I learned how to make this gooey sweet plate of heaven while I was studying in Thailand and absolutely fell in love. Creamy coconut milk is a Thai staple ingredient, and became the sweetness of my soul. Being inspired to make this recipe in 'donut form' was my inner fat kid calling.

Directions:

1. In a rice cooker, cook the sweet rice (glutinous rice) with water.
2. Press the warm rice into donut molds. Chill for a few minutes.
3. Stir together the coconut cream and sweetened condensed milk.
4. Pop the rice donut out of the mold and drizzle with the coconut mixture.
5. Garnish the donut with fresh mango and black sesame seeds.

Ingredients:

2 cups sweet rice

2 cups water

¼ cup coconut cream

2 Tbsp sweetened
condensed milk

1 ripe mango, sliced

2 Tbsp black sesame seeds

Be inspired

Bee Tip: sweet rice, also known as glutinous rice is especially sticky when cooked. It's crucial in this recipe for molding the donut form.

Side Notes

DRESSIEST DRESSINGS

A good dressing is like your favorite t-shirt, when you put it on you never want to take it off. In fact, you want to rock it every day of the week. Creating new dressing combinations is a fun way to recreate your favorite recipes to spice up any day of the week.

By no means do you have to follow any rules when making a dressing, but here's a basic structure I love:

½ vinegar (or other similar tangy acid)

¼ any fat

¼ sweet, spice, or herb

If the ratio is hard to imagine, try starting with one basic recipe like honey balsamic dressing, which includes ½ cup balsamic, ¼ cup olive oil, and ¼ cup honey. To mix up, maybe substitute 1 ripe avocado for half of the olive oil. Now, a revamped, flavor-packed, avocado balsamic dressing. A rainbow collection of my favorite dressings on the next page can perhaps be used for a foundation to your own playground while cooking.

Bee Tip: To make all my dressings, simply blend all the ingredients together on high until smooth except the oil. Slowly whisk in the oil after all the other ingredients are pureed.

Super Ginger :

Super Ginger
1/2 cup rice vinegar
1/4 cup fresh ginger
2 Tbsp dates or brown sugar
2 Tbsp soy sauce
2 Tbsp sesame seeds
1/4 avocado oil

Mighty Green:

1/4 cup apple cider vinegar
1/4 cup lime juice
1 ripe avocado
1 Tbsp fresh mint
1 Tbsp fresh cilantro

Apple Cider :

1/2 cup apple cider
1 Tbsp crushed garlic
1 shallot, minced
2 Tbsp beet juice
1 tsp Dijon
salt, to taste
1/4 cup olive oil

Purple Pesto :

1/4 cup reduced balsamic
vinegar
1/4 cup fresh basil
2 Tbsp pine nuts
2 Tbsp parmesan
1 tsp fresh lavender
1/4 cup olive oil

Lemon Thyme:

1/4 cup apple cider vinegar
1/4 cup lemon juice
1/4 cup pure maple syrup
2-3 Tbsp fresh thyme
1/4 tsp grated nutmeg
1/4 cup canola oil
salt and pepper, to taste

Blueberry BBQ:

1/4 cup frozen blueberries
2 Tbsp brown sugar
2 Tbsp balsamic vinegar
2 Tbsp white vinegar
2 garlic cubes
2 Tbsp yellow onion, diced
1 chipotle pepper in adobo sauce
1/2 tsp cumin
1/4 tsp coffee granules
1/2 tsp chipotle powder
salt and pepper

PLANT POWER

Plants are the core of our life. Trees clean and oxygenate the air we breathe, fields and forests provide a home for all our beautiful wildlife, and nature's ingredients are basis of our own recipes. Simply put, plants are the essence of our livelihood.

For me, looking at the vast variety of edible plants available is overwhelming. Cooking merely with plants will provide you with all the nutrients you need to live. From nuts and seed, to oils and legumes, the Earth is flourishing with food. With a simple rule, if you respect the food you grow, the food will continue to grow and nurture you.

As humans, we're bound to an intimate relationship with mother nature. Old young, rich and poor are holding on dearly to the love it gives us. It only makes sense to keep the love sustainable. In the end, plants and humans come full circle to create our flourishing planet.

All this talk about plants is crucial to the culinary world. An essential part of learning the basics of cooking is noticing the importance of sustainability. Learning how to have fun with whole food ingredients from your local farmers instead of grocery store convenience items makes eating an earned pleasure rather than a quick fix. After all, anytime you use a quick fix, does it ever last forever?

Sustainable cooking includes recognizing the path your food takes to get to you. How respectfully are you taking food from the Earth, are you replenishing it or leaving your trails behind? Knowing how to eat foods kindly from our planet is passing on a colorful culinary path to our future.

WHAT'S IN A RECIPE?

For me, it's love, imagination, and nourishment. In the most basic sense, a recipe is fuel for our bodies. It's our only natural and necessary medicine to keep us alive and strong. That's why building a recipe with wholesome ingredients tastes so satisfying. It's what our bodies crave. Instead of frantically throwing anything together to suppress your hunger, try recognizing what your body needs. More fiber, fats, or minerals? Maybe it's even as simple as water. We often forget to appreciate that we eat for nourishment.

Ingredient Heroes

Whole Grains- quinoa, barley, steel-cut oats, brown rice, whole rye

Power plants- kale, chard, beet greens, spinach, broccolini, tomatoes, mushrooms

Healthy Fats- coconut, avocado, nuts, seeds, olive oil

Detoxifying- ginger, garlic, green tea, lemons, apples, artichokes, seaweed

Breaking down a recipe's structure sets my imagination on fire. Sometimes I like to focus in on one ingredients and build outward to simplify things. For example, start with your favorite ingredient. I'll pick avocados. Now think about their texture, temperature, flavor, color, and nutrients. Every other ingredient added to the recipe thereafter compliments that avocado's personality. I imagined cilantro and salt for more flavor and mushrooms and jalapenos for texture and nutrients. A recipe is like any type of art. You can loosely follow rules, but the real magic happens with your imagination.

Lastly, and most importantly, to create a good recipe, one that you save forever and cherish with your friends, you have to love it. Love isn't something you can actually taste, yet when it's in food, it's one of the most powerful things you can feel. Tasting love in food is noticing the person behind the food, appreciating where the food was grown, why it was created, and who's imagination it represents.

In the end, the best ingredient for cooking is being the best you!

Katie Belanger, author, illustrator, and chef lives a very colorful life through creative arts. While growing up in Chicago, she built her own culinary style from working in the restaurant world for 10 years, earning a degree in business and restaurant management, tasting through endless travels, and never forgetting to be your very best self every step of the way. *The Honey B* is her own quirky, quaint restaurant in Santa Barbara, CA cooking up a unique selection of her homemade recipes. Katie thrives off using plant-based ingredients in unique and innovative ways. Her recipes and paintings alike glow with color, creating irresistible happiness energizing the restaurant. Stimulating her creativity, painting is her yin and cooking is her yang. Katie has also showcased her culinary creativity, winning TNT's cooking show *On The Menu* along with featuring The Honey B waffles on *Haley's America* on The Food Channel. She's also been seen on local cooking channels. The *Be You Cookbook* is based off the happy life Katie likes to live by; "Spread the love of cooking to encourage creativity within yourself!"

BE YOU!
COOKBOOK

Acknowledgments:
Author & Illustrations by Katie Belanger
Photography by Rob LaFond and Vincent Brock